by Arthur Zaidenberg

How to Draw

HEADS and FACES

Abelard-Schuman
New York

BOOKS BY ARTHUR ZAIDENBERG

How to Draw Ballet and Other Dancers
How to Draw Birds, Fish and Reptiles
How to Draw a Circus
How to Draw and Compose Pictures
How to Draw Costumes and Clothes
How to Draw Dogs, Cats and Horses
How to Draw Farm Animals
How to Draw Heads and Faces
How to Draw Houses
How to Draw Landscapes, Seascapes and Cityscapes
How to Draw Military and Civilian Uniforms
How to Draw Motors, Machines and Tools
How to Draw Musicians and Musical Instruments
How to Draw People at Work
How to Draw Period Costumes
How to Draw Shakespeare's People
How to Draw the Wild West
How to Draw Wild Animals

Printed in the United States of America

L.C. Card AC 66-10314
ISBN 0-200-71813-4 RB

8   9   10

Contents

Introduction

For an artist, nothing in nature holds an interest comparable to that of the human face. The drama of sunsets, the beauty of flowers, the excitement of the sea and the majesty and menace of mountain peaks all hold intense fascination for the artist. But his response to the ever-changing, emotional "theatre" presented by human features can never be matched.

The range of expression of which the face of a sensitive human being is capable has always been a challenge to the artist. The greatest of artists have only been able to capture a facsimile of these vital expressions, at best, leaving infinitely more to be said. Emotions—such as anger, joy and love—expressed by the human eye or silent lips, are only registered in relatively static, inadequate "shorthand" by the artist's pencil. Since the beginning of time, however, artists have been absorbed in trying to capture even some of these fleeting emotions.

Because the artist can only hope to simulate an arrested moment of expression, he must find means of intensifying that vital moment. This he does by eliminating all detail which does not contribute to such expression, and *that is* the challenging and absorbing game played by the artist.

In these pages, we shall try to prepare the student with some fundamental knowledge of form of the head and features in action, so that he may be equipped to play that delightful game of drawing the living, breathing, thinking and feeling facial expressions.

Beyond that, this book cannot hope to go. The student must continue throughout his artistic lifetime to observe, understand and "feel," adding to these indispensable activities the practice necessary to develop his knowledge of drawing. Then, as he develops skills with the materials of the artist, he will learn to draw living faces which "say things" to the beholder.

Materials Used in This Book

Most of the drawings in this book were done with a carbon pencil. Buy several of them—ranging from soft to medium—from an art-supply shop. Also buy a kneaded rubber for erasures, but use it sparingly!

Some of the drawings were made with pen and India ink. A few were done with a watercolor brush and India ink. But you need not restrict yourself to the drawing materials mentioned here. There are many other types you can use, and all artists experiment until they find the drawing materials best suited to their needs.

Get a small sketchbook to keep in your pocket. For drawing at home, there are many varieties of textured drawing paper available. Try several different types—each has its own virtues.

HEAD SHAPE

The form of the head is essentially egg-shaped. The features, except for the protruding nose, lie quite close to the egg form and disturb its shape very little.

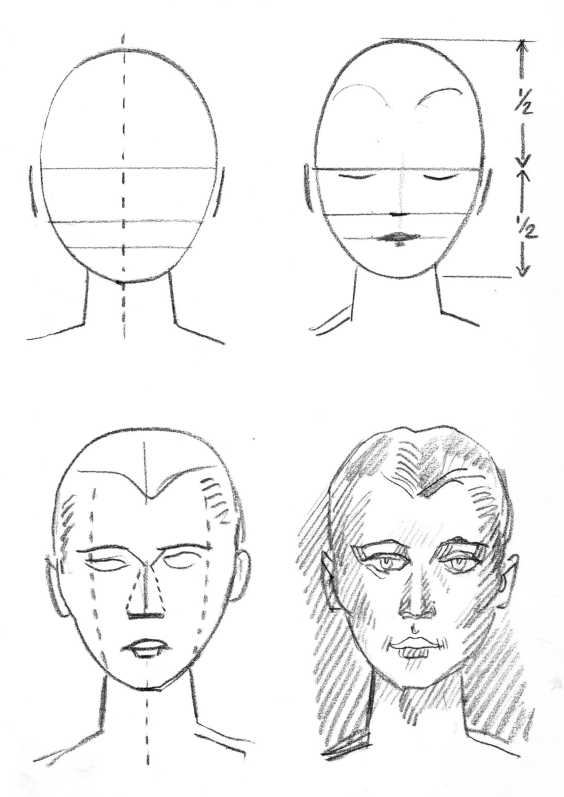

THE PLACING OF FEATURES

In the beginning, students find it more difficult to draw a full face than a profile. They carefully trace the outline of the profile, defining it on the paper as a silhouette, with no suggestion of solid form of either the features or the head. Actually, it seems more difficult to draw this delicate outline with any degree of resemblance to the living features and head than it is to "construct" the forms of the features, and place them on and in the solid form of the skull. Examine the shape of the human skull and notice how its features lie within settings reserved for them.

The features follow
the orbit around the
turning form of the
head shape.

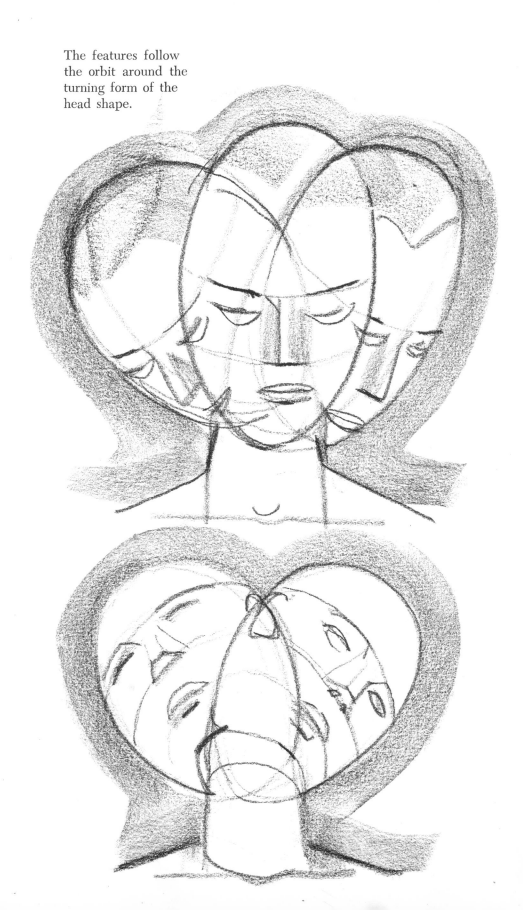

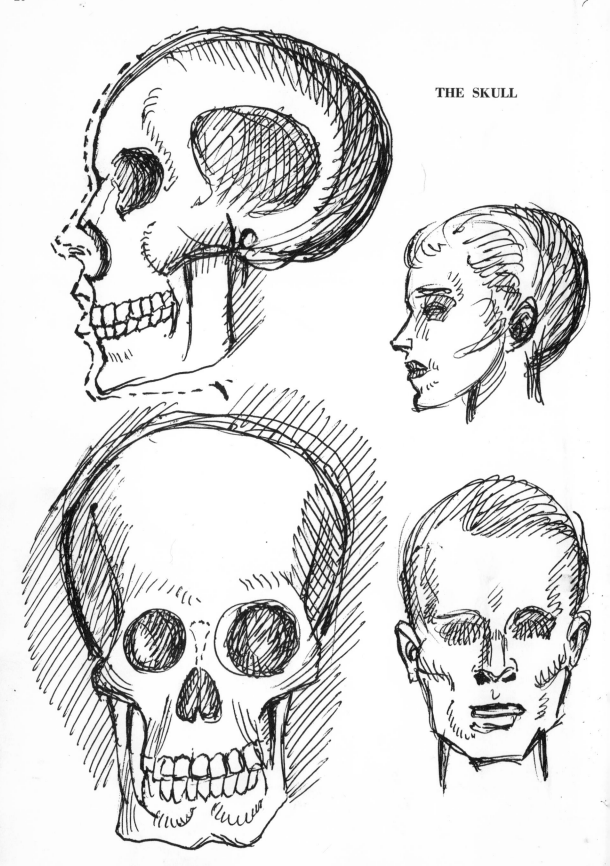

THE SKULL

PROPORTIONS

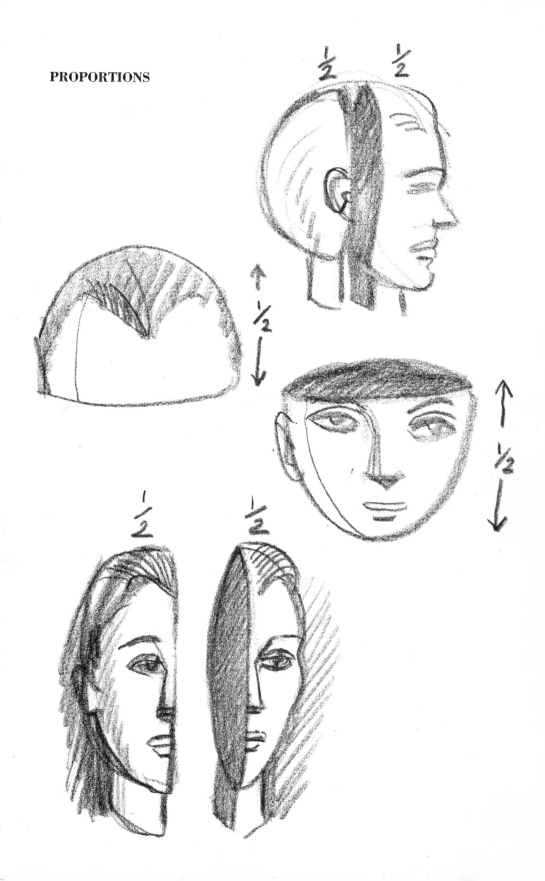

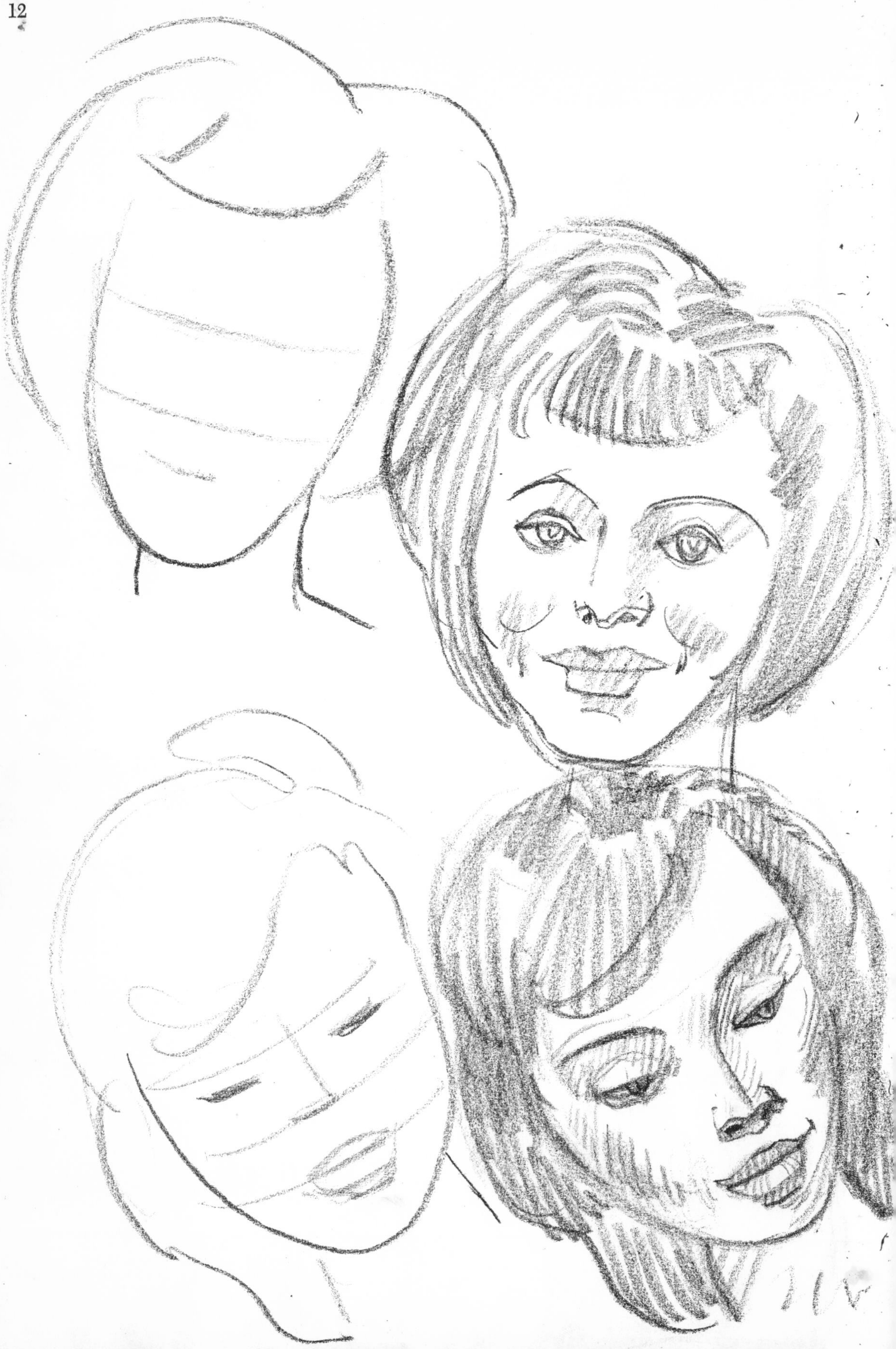

THE NOSE
The nose form seems quite complex, but it really
can be built with a simple wedge-shaped form.

THE MOUTH

Study the changes in the character of the mouth, in its many moods. You cannot make the lips you draw speak, of course, but you can make them express a great range of feeling.

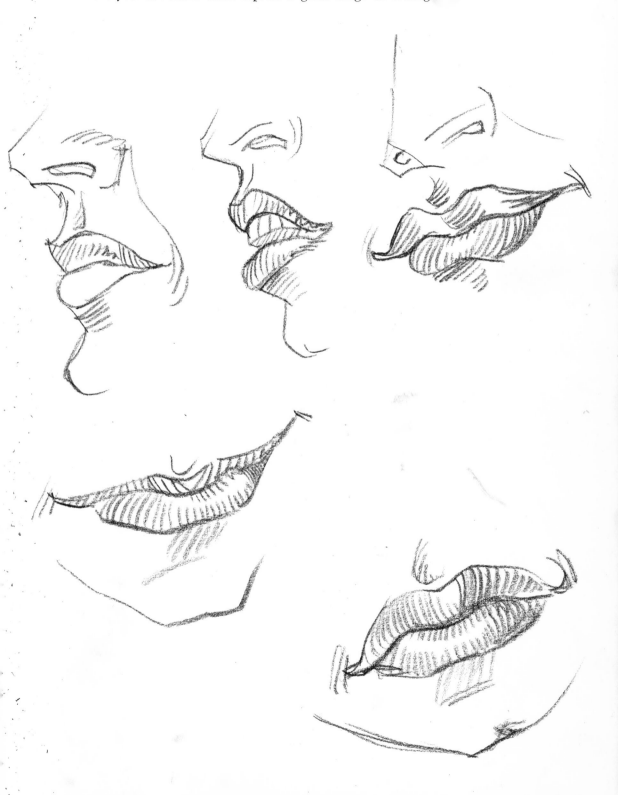

THE EYE

In drawing the eye, a common mistake is overemphasizing the pupil and neglecting other structural areas which contribute so much to its expression and character.

Study these simplified constructions of the total eye and eye areas.

Draw your own eyes in the mirror from every position.

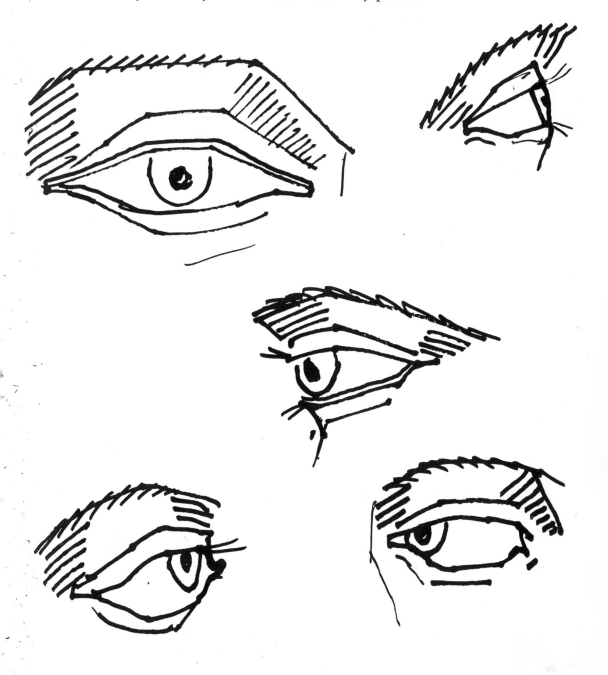

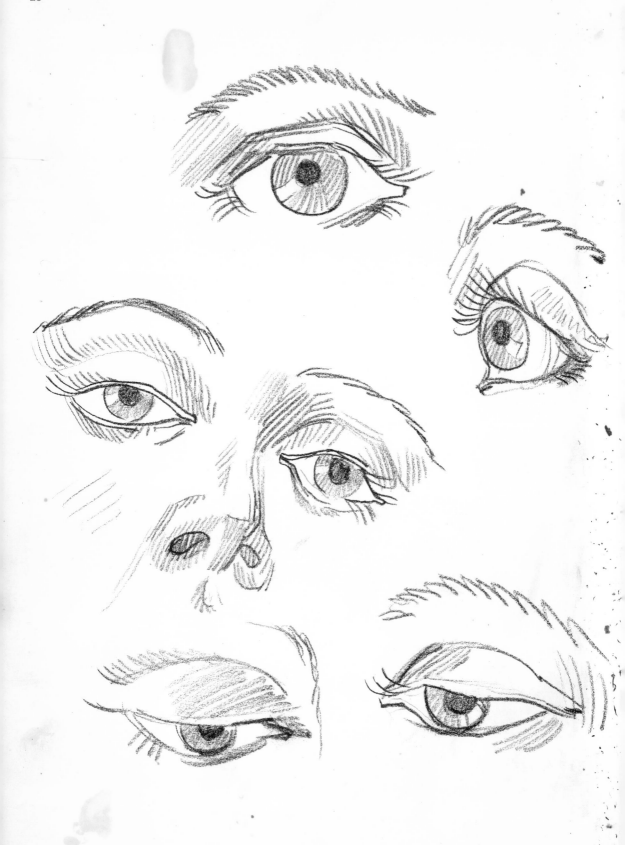

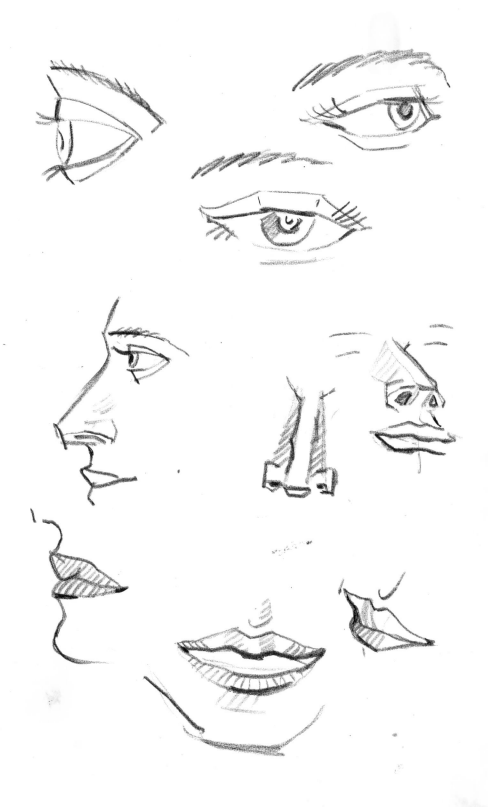

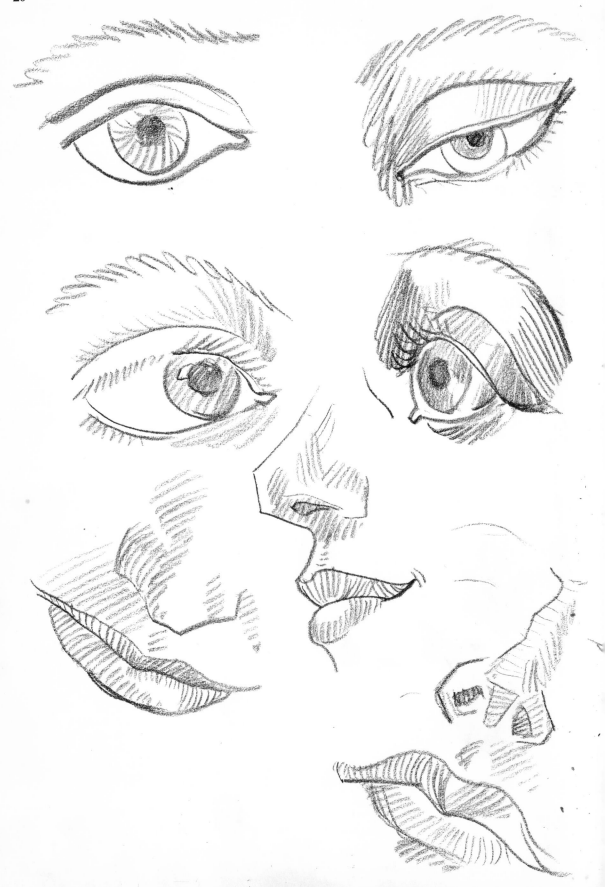

THE EAR

THE NECK
Place the head on a sturdy, simple
column, which is the essential
character of the neck.

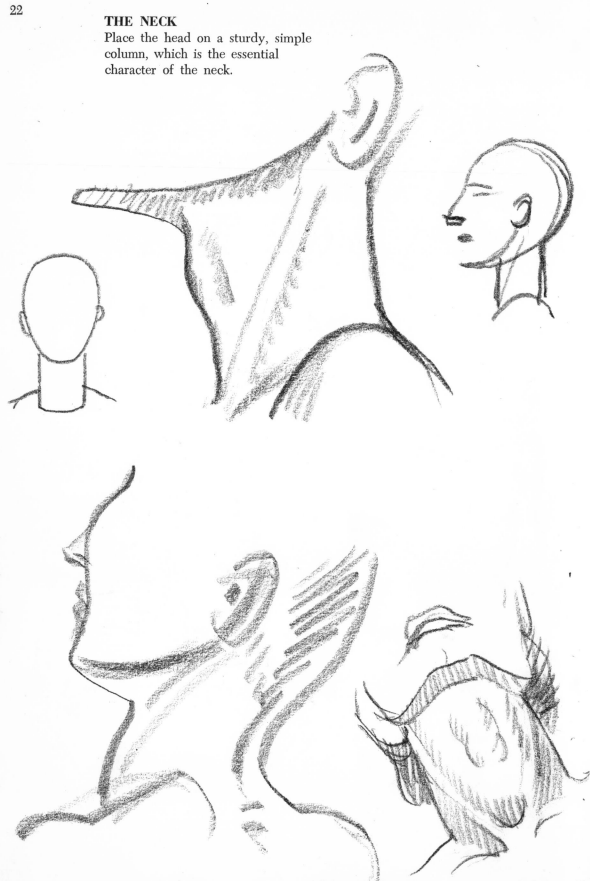

PATTERNS OF SHADOWS
This head is a study of the shapes of shadows.
Pose for yourself before a mirror and study the
shadows thrown on your face.
Make a careful outline pattern drawing of the
main shadows.

Here, the patterns of the shadows have been filled in as evenly as possible with pencil strokes all slanting in the same direction. Fill in the large, lighter shadows first—then the smaller, darker ones, leaving the white paper to suggest unshaded, lighted areas.

Structural lines for the sculpturelike
drawings of four heads.

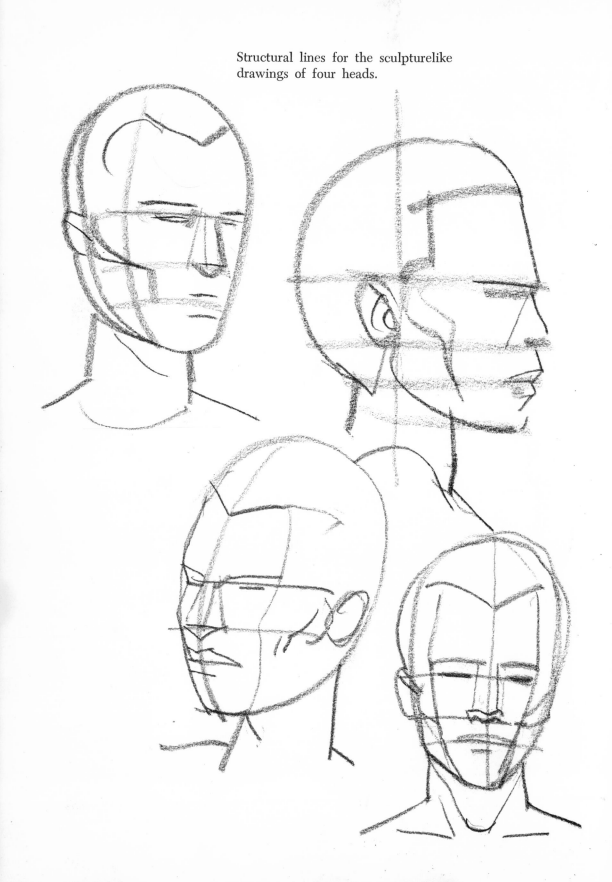

Another shadow-pattern study, ready for
filling in with the tones of the shadows.

In this case, the lines of shading to fill in the shadow patterns follow the contours of the facial forms.

CONTRAST STUDIES
Notice how just those two large
contrasting areas of light and shade
convey the form of the complete head.

Here, the forms have been suggested by strong contrast between the blocks of black ink and the clean white paper. Notice how much can be said with those simple blocks.

Find the source of light cast
upon a face, and notice how the
areas turned away from that light
are almost lost in shadows.

Drawing heads from sculpture
pieces is very good practice.
The model poses without movement,
and the simplification has
already been performed for you
by the sculptor.

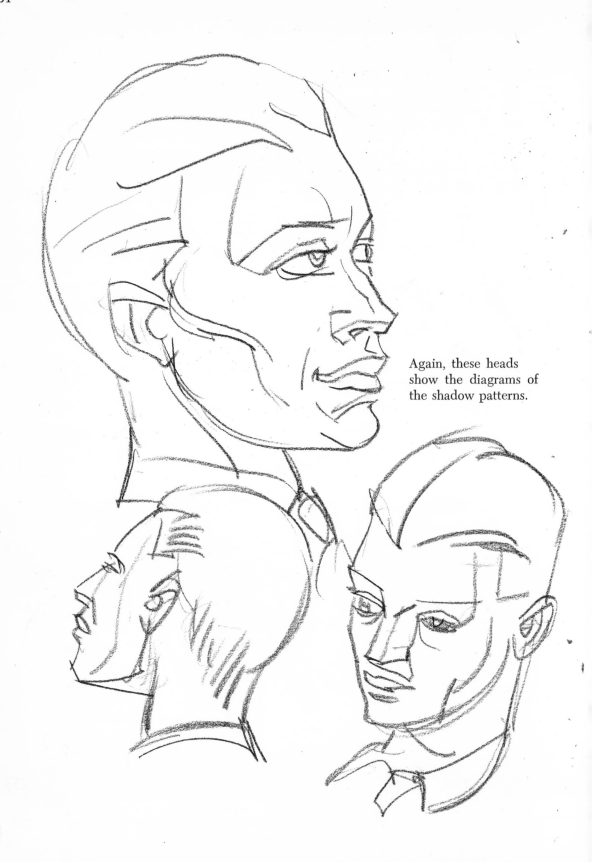

Again, these heads show the diagrams of the shadow patterns.

EVEN-TONE SHADING
The filling in of the shadow patterns on these heads was
done with carefully drawn, even tones rather than open lines.

SMILES AND LAUGHTER
Smiles and laughter produce certain typical wrinkles in all
faces, and the egg-shaped oval of the face seems to broaden.

PAIN, FEAR AND SURPRISE
Misery and pain seem to make the face longer, and make the
features and wrinkles droop.
Surprise rounds the eyes, arches the eyebrows and seems to
make the mouth say "oooh!"

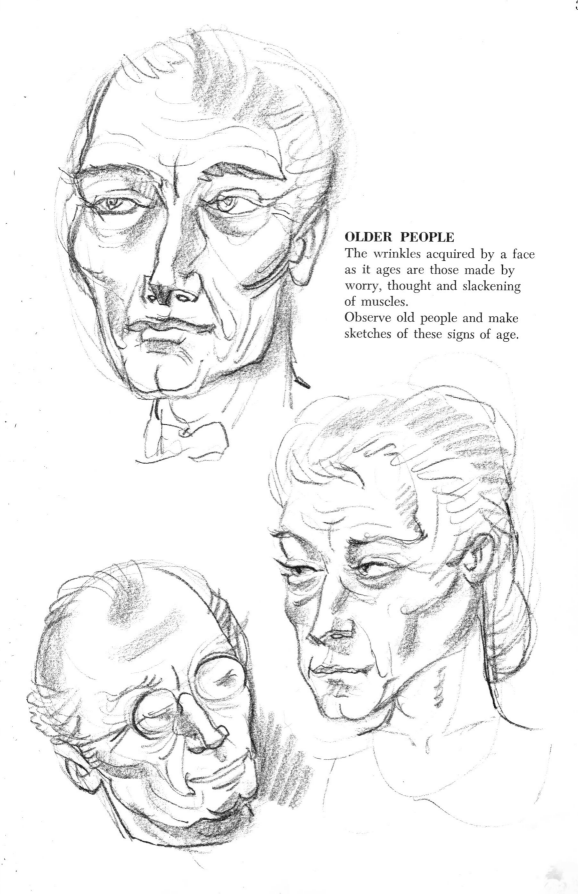

OLDER PEOPLE

The wrinkles acquired by a face as it ages are those made by worry, thought and slackening of muscles.

Observe old people and make sketches of these signs of age.

CHILDREN
Children's faces are relatively large and round, while the features are tiny and also tend to be round.

BEARDS

The wide variety of beards worn these days are fun to draw. Make a habit of sketching the different ones you see.

HAIR
Study the wide variety of ways in which hair is worn and draw the general, over-all shape of the hair rather than thousands of individual hairs.

RACIAL TYPES

Study the various types of facial structure of people of different races as they sit opposite you in a train or bus, or pass you on the street. You will find much beauty in these faces if you examine and draw them with sympathy and interest.

HALF-HEAD EXERCISES

Copy these half-drawings and finish them carefully, noting the proportions and placement of the features in relation to each other. Then, without referring to the drawings, try to draw similar heads on another sheet of paper. When you have finished, check back and see how well you have done.

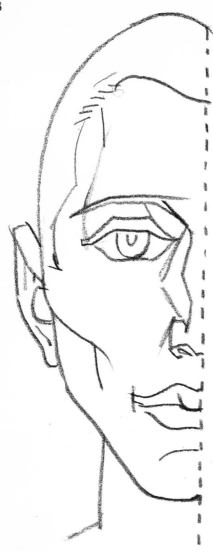

50

"WRITTEN" FACES

The following exercises in "writing" faces are presented, not as a trick, but as a legitimate method of getting more "play" into your drawings.

The gay vitality of script, which you have learned to use spontaneously and flowingly, gives a bright freshness to these faces. Try "writing" a few similar faces. First, make a very light outline drawing of a face and features. Then write directly over those light lines with your fountain pen.

BRUSH AND INDIA INK DRAWINGS
Very freely drawn, quick-sketch brush
and India ink drawings. Try some.

SCRIBBLED LINES

Practice "scribbled line" drawings, using a fountain pen or a crow quill drawing pen which has a very fine point and is used with India ink. Such practice will develop freedom in your drawings, and help soften the hard geometric forms with which you have been constructing your earlier drawings.

CONTINUOUS-LINE DRAWINGS

These heads were drawn with one continuous line, without lifting the pen from the paper.

Try drawing some heads using a continuous line with your pencil or pen. You will find that this exercise will improve the free flow of your drawing.

SHORT-LINE DRAWINGS

Here are some heads drawn with short lines. Almost all of the lines are of the same thickness, made with the same pressure on the pen.

Drawings made in this manner rely on the sensitive "wave" of the line to suggest form.

DRAWINGS WITH FELT-POINT MARKING PENS

These heads were drawn with felt-point marking pens, which are sold every-where. Although the pens are rather heavy and blunt, and unsuited to fine detail work, they help simplify and strengthen drawings which have been produced with fine-pointed pencils and have become overrefined.

BRUSH STROKES

Try drawing some heads, using a brush and ink. Make your brush strokes swiftly, but thoughtfully, and do not try to put in too much detail.

HEADS DRAWN FROM THE WORK OF GREAT ARTISTS

On this, and the following two pages, are heads drawn from the work of six great artists.

Study their own special approach to drawing faces. Each has a very personal viewpoint.

Make *your* drawings of faces express what *you* think and feel about them.

AFTER MATISSE

AFTER VAN GOGH

AFTER A DRAWING BY
PETER PAUL RUBENS OF
HIS SON, NICOLAS, IN 162

AFTER PAUL KLEE

L'ARLESIENNE

AFTER PAUL GAUGUIN

HEAD OF A WOMAN
TOULOUSE-LAUTREC

Final Word

We have drawn many faces together in these pages, and now you must go on, on your own. You can be sure that your interest in faces will never wane. For each face one sees is different and tells a different story. When you can draw a face and tell its story, those who see your drawings will share it with you.

Look keenly at the faces about you.

Study their character and their moods.

Sketch them—all of them.

You will find great pleasure in doing this, and you may give great pleasure to others.